T0346577

Yacht Log

Of the Vessel

NAVIGATION.

The great End & Business of Navigation is to instruct the Mariner how to conduct a Ship through the wide & pathless Ocean, to the remotest Parts of the World, the safest & shortest Way, in Passages navigable.

The Mariner's   Compass.

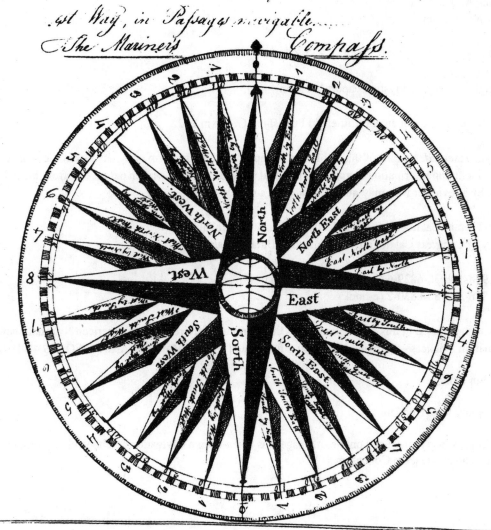

LYONS PRESS/MYSTIC SEAPORT MUSEUM
Guilford Connecticut

Lyons Press/Mystic Seaport Museum
An imprint of Globe Pequot, the Trade Division of The Rowman & Littlefield Publishing Group, Inc.
4501 Forbes Blvd., Ste. 200
Lanham, MD 20706
www.rowman.com

Distributed by NATIONAL BOOK NETWORK

British Library Cataloguing in Publication Information available
Library of Congress Cataloging-in-Publication Data available

ISBN 978-1-4930-6829-6 (hardcover: alk. paper)
ISBN 978-1-4930-6830-2 (e-book)

♾™ The paper used in this publication meets the minimum requirements of American National Standard for Information Sciences—Permanence of Paper for Printed Library Materials, ANSI/NISO Z39.48-1992.

Printed in India

Designed by Kate Hemlen

The compass rose reproduced on the title page was taken from a navigation notebook circa 1785, in the Mystic Seaport Museum Collection.

Sailing Year _____

Yacht Name _____

Owner _____

Documentation or Registration Number _____

Hailing Port _____

Radio Call Letters _____

Type or Class _____

Yacht Data

Hull Number _____

L.O.A. _____

L.W.L. _____

Beam _____

Draft _____

    C.B. Down _____

Docking Length _____

Power Requirements _____

Mast Height Above W.L. _____

Sail Number _____

Engine Model _____

    Series _____

    Serial No. _____

Propeller Data _____

    Size _____

    Pitch _____

Electronic Equipment _____

    R.D.F. _____

    LORAN _____

    V.H.F. _____

    S.S.B. _____

    Depth Sounder _____

    Other _____

_____

_____

Dinghy or Inflatable _____

    Hull Number _____

    Registration No. _____

Outboard Motor _____

    Model _____

    Serial No. _____

Life Raft _____

    Serial No. _____

Compass _____

    Model Number _____

    Serial Number _____

_____

Sundry Gear _____

_____

_____

How to Use this Yacht Log by Kenneth Mahler

Like many other yachtsmen, I have purchased commercially printed logbooks on numerous occasions. Frustration with the failings of these logs forced me to design a simple, inexpensive log for my own use. Hearing of my persistence in maintaining a log aboard my Nat Herreshoff sloop MASHNEE and as a member of the staff at the Seaport, the Mystic Seaport Museum Stores requested my help in designing a new logbook for yachtsmen.

Conscious that my own ideas should not be the only resource, I inspected a number of logs, both contemporary and those in our museum collection. I spoke with several yachtsmen, navigators and skippers. Reviewing the information I had compiled, I quickly found that no two parties agreed on all elements of a logbook, and that boat owners often modified any commercial log they used. However, this collective experience helped me to select the elements that I trust will make this new log complete and useful for both sail and power boats.

Preserving your memories, recalling the details of idyllic or stormy passages, remembering cruises spent with your favorite guests and recording the important data of your vessel in one convenient location are only a few of the reasons for keeping a log. The conscientious log keeper becomes a favored client for insurance companies and an impressive witness before the Coast Guard, should an incident occur. Certainly the task of keeping a log is a bit of a chore, but in the months and years to come your effort will be rewarded by the benefits of your ability to recall your passages aboard.

Your new log opens with several pages for recording pertinent data about your vessel. Having your yacht's details conveniently at hand becomes particularly helpful when reporting theft, working with a maintenance crew or manufacturer or docking in unfamiliar or crowded ports.

A page is supplied for your guests to sign. The blank column is not headed, so your guests may feel free to write their comments if they choose. You may wish to use the column for noting their favorite drink or meal. Experience dictates a simple rule regarding who should sign the guest page: if they are aboard for more than fifteen minutes guests should be asked to sign the log, and they need do so only once a season. This excuses the brief visitor and avoids multiple signatures of the frequent visitor.

The body of the log contains the pages to record your passages from one port to another. We have added enough room for you to elaborate on your trip under the Remarks column.

We have added important columns for you to note in quick fashion relevant facts of your vessel's operation and the environment. The Navigator's and Skipper's Choice columns have been included for those who need a column for LORAN, trim tabs, RPM, generator operation, charts used, or a dozen other possible notations not necessarily relevant to all boats.

We have kept some of the columns narrow. Again, experience has shown that initials and abbreviations are more convenient than writing out entire words. For example, use initials for the person at the helm. Write NW for northwest. Use the Beaufort Scale printed below for wind force. The current and its direction can be recorded as E for ebb and F for flood. You might wish to use only four conditions of weather: Excl., Good, Poor, and Rain or Snow. The sky can be Blue, Ptly. Cldy., or Grey.

The column for Engine or Sail Combination allows you to note and easily recall your best condition or sail combination under certain circumstances. Your remarks can be as brief or as long as you see fit. We have added a light line between the heavier lines for those entries on which you wish to elaborate.

For those who need reminders, a space has been added on the bottom of the page for this purpose. We have also provided two blanks to note fuel and water taken on for boats with more than one tank. Be sure to list the Persons on Board for your passages. This column will give you an instant P.O.B. report for Coast Guard inquiries or help to identify guests aboard for certain trips.

Finally, we have supplied a complete Radio Log page. By law you are required to report transmissions from your vessel. For those who frequently use the marine radio operators, the radio log provides a clear record to check your bills against and, in retrospect, gives you some idea what operators can or cannot be reached from certain ports. Simple blanks for check marks allow you to note whether your transmission was on high or low power and whether each call was initiated or received by your vessel. The column for the radio call letters of the vessel called can be used to record phone numbers when calls are placed through marine operators.

If you have any suggestions for improvements to this log based on your own experiences, please write to me, care of Mystic Seaport Museum, so that we may refine this log to meet the needs of all boat owners.

Safe and fine yachting.

Kenneth Mahler

Beaufort Scale

Wind Velocity in Knots	Beaufort Scale Number
None	0
1–3	1
4–6	2
7–10	3
11–16	4
17–21	5
22–27	6
28–33	7
34–40	8
41–47	9
48–55	10
56–63	11
64–71	12

Register of Guests

DATE	NAME	FROM VESSEL	HOME

Register of Guests

DATE	NAME	FROM VESSEL	HOME	

Register of Guests

DATE	NAME	FROM VESSEL	HOME

Register of Guests

Register of Guests

DATE	NAME	FROM VESSEL	HOME

Register of Guests

DATE	NAME	FROM VESSEL	HOME

Register of Guests

DATE	NAME	FROM VESSEL	HOME

Log of the Yacht _____ Day of the week _____ Date _____

TIME	POSITION	COURSE	NAVIGATOR'S CHOICE	PERSON AT HELM	SKIPPER'S CHOICE	CURRENT	WIND		WEATHER				
							Dir	Force	Barometer	Conditions	Sky	Vis	Temp

Maintenance and Reminders _____ Fuel taken on _____ gals _____ gals

Water taken on _____ gals _____ gals

Passage from _____ **to** _____

ENGINE OR SAIL COMBINATION	REMARKS, COMMENTS, AND OBSERVATIONS

Persons on board _____

Log of the Yacht _____ Day of the week _____ Date _____

TIME	POSITION	COURSE	NAVIGATOR'S CHOICE	PERSON AT HELM	SKIPPER'S CHOICE	CURRENT	WIND		WEATHER				
							Dir	Force	Barometer	Conditions	Sky	Vis	Temp

Maintenance and Reminders _____

_____

Fuel taken on _____ gals _____ gals

Water taken on _____ gals _____ gals

Passage from _____ **to** _____

ENGINE OR SAIL COMBINATION	REMARKS, COMMENTS, AND OBSERVATIONS

Persons on board _____

Log of the Yacht _____ Day of the week _____ Date _____

TIME	POSITION	COURSE	NAVIGATOR'S CHOICE	PERSON AT HELM	SKIPPER'S CHOICE	CURRENT	WIND		WEATHER				
							Dir	Force	Barometer	Conditions	Sky	Vis	Temp

Maintenance and Reminders _____   Fuel taken on _____ gals _____ gals

_____   Water taken on _____ gals _____ gals

Passage from _____ **to** _____

ENGINE OR SAIL COMBINATION	REMARKS, COMMENTS, AND OBSERVATIONS

Persons on board _____

Log of the Yacht _____ Day of the week _____ Date _____

TIME	POSITION	COURSE	NAVIGATOR'S CHOICE	PERSON AT HELM	SKIPPER'S CHOICE	CURRENT	WIND		WEATHER				
							Dir	Force	Barometer	Conditions	Sky	Vis	Temp

Maintenance and Reminders _____ Fuel taken on _____ gals _____ gals

_____ Water taken on _____ gals _____ gals

Passage from _____ **to** _____

ENGINE OR SAIL COMBINATION	REMARKS, COMMENTS, AND OBSERVATIONS

Persons on board _____

Log of the Yacht _____ Day of the week _____ Date _____

TIME	POSITION	COURSE	NAVIGATOR'S CHOICE	PERSON AT HELM	SKIPPER'S CHOICE	CURRENT	WIND		WEATHER				
							Dir	Force	Barometer	Conditions	Sky	Vis	Temp

Maintenance and Reminders _____   Fuel taken on _____ gals _____ gals

_____   Water taken on _____ gals _____ gals

Passage from _____ **to** _____

ENGINE OR SAIL COMBINATION	REMARKS, COMMENTS, AND OBSERVATIONS

Persons on board _____

Log of the Yacht _____ Day of the week _____ Date _____

TIME	POSITION	COURSE	NAVIGATOR'S CHOICE	PERSON AT HELM	SKIPPER'S CHOICE	CURRENT	WIND		WEATHER				
							Dir	Force	Barometer	Conditions	Sky	Vis	Temp

Maintenance and Reminders _____   Fuel taken on _____ gals _____ gals

_____   Water taken on _____ gals _____ gals

Passage from _____ **to** _____

ENGINE OR SAIL COMBINATION	REMARKS, COMMENTS, AND OBSERVATIONS

Persons on board _____

Log of the Yacht _____ Day of the week _____ Date _____

TIME	POSITION	COURSE	NAVIGATOR'S CHOICE	PERSON AT HELM	SKIPPER'S CHOICE	CURRENT	WIND		WEATHER				
							Dir	Force	Barometer	Conditions	Sky	Vis	Temp

Maintenance and Reminders _____ Fuel taken on _____ gals _____ gals

_____ Water taken on _____ gals _____ gals

Passage from _____ **to** _____

ENGINE OR SAIL COMBINATION	REMARKS, COMMENTS, AND OBSERVATIONS

Persons on board _____

Log of the Yacht _____ Day of the week _____ Date _____

TIME	POSITION	COURSE	NAVIGATOR'S CHOICE	PERSON AT HELM	SKIPPER'S CHOICE	CURRENT	WIND		WEATHER				
							Dir	Force	Barometer	Conditions	Sky	Vis	Temp

Maintenance and Reminders _____

Fuel taken on _____ gals _____ gals

Water taken on _____ gals _____ gals

Passage from _____ **to** _____

ENGINE OR SAIL COMBINATION	REMARKS, COMMENTS, AND OBSERVATIONS

Persons on board _____

Log of the Yacht _____ Day of the week _____ Date _____

TIME	POSITION	COURSE	NAVIGATOR'S CHOICE	PERSON AT HELM	SKIPPER'S CHOICE	CURRENT	WIND		WEATHER				
							Dir	Force	Barometer	Conditions	Sky	Vis	Temp

Maintenance and Reminders _____

_____

Fuel taken on _____ gals _____ gals

Water taken on _____ gals _____ gals

Passage from _____ **to** _____

ENGINE OR SAIL COMBINATION	REMARKS, COMMENTS, AND OBSERVATIONS

Persons on board _____

Log of the Yacht _____ Day of the week _____ Date _____

TIME	POSITION	COURSE	NAVIGATOR'S CHOICE	PERSON AT HELM	SKIPPER'S CHOICE	CURRENT	WIND		WEATHER				
							Dir	Force	Barometer	Conditions	Sky	Vis	Temp

Maintenance and Reminders _____   Fuel taken on _____ gals _____ gals

_____   Water taken on _____ gals _____ gals

Passage from _____ **to** _____

ENGINE OR SAIL COMBINATION	REMARKS, COMMENTS, AND OBSERVATIONS

Persons on board _____

Log of the Yacht _____ Day of the week _____ Date _____

TIME	POSITION	COURSE	NAVIGATOR'S CHOICE	PERSON AT HELM	SKIPPER'S CHOICE	CURRENT	WIND		WEATHER				
							Dir	Force	Barometer	Conditions	Sky	Vis	Temp

Maintenance and Reminders _____   Fuel taken on _____ gals _____ gals

_____   Water taken on _____ gals _____ gals

Passage from _____ **to** _____

ENGINE OR SAIL COMBINATION	REMARKS, COMMENTS, AND OBSERVATIONS

Persons on board _____

Log of the Yacht _____ Day of the week _____ Date _____

TIME	POSITION	COURSE	NAVIGATOR'S CHOICE	PERSON AT HELM	SKIPPER'S CHOICE	CURRENT	WIND		WEATHER				
							Dir	Force	Barometer	Conditions	Sky	Vis	Temp

Maintenance and Reminders _____ Fuel taken on _____ gals _____ gals

_____ Water taken on _____ gals _____ gals

Passage from _____ **to** _____

ENGINE OR SAIL COMBINATION	REMARKS, COMMENTS, AND OBSERVATIONS

Persons on board _____

Log of the Yacht _____ Day of the week _____ Date _____

TIME	POSITION	COURSE	NAVIGATOR'S CHOICE	PERSON AT HELM	SKIPPER'S CHOICE	CURRENT	WIND		WEATHER				
							Dir	Force	Barometer	Conditions	Sky	Vis	Temp

Maintenance and Reminders _____ Fuel taken on _____ gals _____ gals

_____ Water taken on _____ gals _____ gals

Passage from _____ **to** _____

ENGINE OR SAIL COMBINATION	REMARKS, COMMENTS, AND OBSERVATIONS

Persons on board _____

Log of the Yacht _____ Day of the week _____ Date _____

TIME	POSITION	COURSE	NAVIGATOR'S CHOICE	PERSON AT HELM	SKIPPER'S CHOICE	CURRENT	WIND		WEATHER				
							Dir	Force	Barometer	Conditions	Sky	Vis	Temp

Maintenance and Reminders _____ Fuel taken on _____ gals _____ gals

_____ Water taken on _____ gals _____ gals

Passage from _____ **to** _____

ENGINE OR SAIL COMBINATION	REMARKS, COMMENTS, AND OBSERVATIONS

Persons on board _____

Log of the Yacht _____ Day of the week _____ Date _____

TIME	POSITION	COURSE	NAVIGATOR'S CHOICE	PERSON AT HELM	SKIPPER'S CHOICE	CURRENT	WIND		WEATHER				
							Dir	Force	Barometer	Conditions	Sky	Vis	Temp

Maintenance and Reminders _____ Fuel taken on _____ gals _____ gals

_____ Water taken on _____ gals _____ gals

Passage from _____ **to** _____

ENGINE OR SAIL COMBINATION	REMARKS, COMMENTS, AND OBSERVATIONS

Persons on board _____

Log of the Yacht _____ Day of the week _____ Date _____

TIME	POSITION	COURSE	NAVIGATOR'S CHOICE	PERSON AT HELM	SKIPPER'S CHOICE	CURRENT	WIND		WEATHER				
							Dir	Force	Barometer	Conditions	Sky	Vis	Temp

Maintenance and Reminders _____ Fuel taken on _____ gals _____ gals

_____ Water taken on _____ gals _____ gals

Passage from _____ **to** _____

ENGINE OR SAIL COMBINATION	REMARKS, COMMENTS, AND OBSERVATIONS

Persons on board _____

Log of the Yacht _____ Day of the week _____ Date _____

TIME	POSITION	COURSE	NAVIGATOR'S CHOICE	PERSON AT HELM	SKIPPER'S CHOICE	CURRENT	WIND		WEATHER				
							Dir	Force	Barometer	Conditions	Sky	Vis	Temp

Maintenance and Reminders _____

Fuel taken on _____ gals _____ gals

Water taken on _____ gals _____ gals

Passage from _____ **to** _____

ENGINE OR SAIL COMBINATION	REMARKS, COMMENTS, AND OBSERVATIONS

Persons on board _____

Log of the Yacht _____ Day of the week _____ Date _____

TIME	POSITION	COURSE	NAVIGATOR'S CHOICE	PERSON AT HELM	SKIPPER'S CHOICE	CURRENT	WIND		WEATHER				
							Dir	Force	Barometer	Conditions	Sky	Vis	Temp

Maintenance and Reminders _____   Fuel taken on _____ gals _____ gals

_____   Water taken on _____ gals _____ gals

Passage from _____ **to** _____

ENGINE OR SAIL COMBINATION	REMARKS, COMMENTS, AND OBSERVATIONS

Persons on board _____

Log of the Yacht _____ Day of the week _____ Date _____

TIME	POSITION	COURSE	NAVIGATOR'S CHOICE	PERSON AT HELM	SKIPPER'S CHOICE	CURRENT	WIND		WEATHER				
							Dir	Force	Barometer	Conditions	Sky	Vis	Temp

Maintenance and Reminders _____ Fuel taken on _____ gals _____ gals

_____ Water taken on _____ gals _____ gals

Passage from _____ **to** _____

ENGINE OR SAIL COMBINATION	REMARKS, COMMENTS, AND OBSERVATIONS

Persons on board _____

Log of the Yacht _____ Day of the week _____ Date _____

TIME	POSITION	COURSE	NAVIGATOR'S CHOICE	PERSON AT HELM	SKIPPER'S CHOICE	CURRENT	WIND		WEATHER				
							Dir	Force	Barometer	Conditions	Sky	Vis	Temp

Maintenance and Reminders _____ Fuel taken on _____ gals _____ gals

_____ Water taken on _____ gals _____ gals

Passage from _____ **to** _____

ENGINE OR SAIL COMBINATION	REMARKS, COMMENTS, AND OBSERVATIONS

Persons on board _____

Log of the Yacht _____ Day of the week _____ Date _____

TIME	POSITION	COURSE	NAVIGATOR'S CHOICE	PERSON AT HELM	SKIPPER'S CHOICE	CURRENT	WIND		WEATHER				
							Dir	Force	Barometer	Conditions	Sky	Vis	Temp

Maintenance and Reminders _____   Fuel taken on _____ gals _____ gals

_____   Water taken on _____ gals _____ gals

Passage from _____ **to** _____

ENGINE OR SAIL COMBINATION	REMARKS, COMMENTS, AND OBSERVATIONS

Persons on board _____

Log of the Yacht _____ Day of the week _____ Date _____

TIME	POSITION	COURSE	NAVIGATOR'S CHOICE	PERSON AT HELM	SKIPPER'S CHOICE	CURRENT	WIND		WEATHER				
							Dir	Force	Barometer	Conditions	Sky	Vis	Temp

Maintenance and Reminders _____

_____

Fuel taken on _____ gals _____ gals

Water taken on _____ gals _____ gals

Passage from _____ **to** _____

ENGINE OR SAIL COMBINATION	REMARKS, COMMENTS, AND OBSERVATIONS

Persons on board _____

Log of the Yacht _____ Day of the week _____ Date _____

TIME	POSITION	COURSE	NAVIGATOR'S CHOICE	PERSON AT HELM	SKIPPER'S CHOICE	CURRENT	WIND		WEATHER				
							Dir	Force	Barometer	Conditions	Sky	Vis	Temp

Maintenance and Reminders _____ Fuel taken on _____ gals _____ gals

_____ Water taken on _____ gals _____ gals

Passage from _____ **to** _____

ENGINE OR SAIL COMBINATION	REMARKS, COMMENTS, AND OBSERVATIONS

Persons on board _____

Log of the Yacht _____ Day of the week _____ Date _____

TIME	POSITION	COURSE	NAVIGATOR'S CHOICE	PERSON AT HELM	SKIPPER'S CHOICE	CURRENT	WIND		WEATHER				
							Dir	Force	Barometer	Conditions	Sky	Vis	Temp

Maintenance and Reminders _____ Fuel taken on _____ gals _____ gals

_____ Water taken on _____ gals _____ gals

Passage from _____ **to** _____

ENGINE OR SAIL COMBINATION	REMARKS, COMMENTS, AND OBSERVATIONS

Persons on board _____

Log of the Yacht

Day of the week _____ Date _____

TIME	POSITION	COURSE	NAVIGATOR'S CHOICE	PERSON AT HELM	SKIPPER'S CHOICE	CURRENT	WIND		WEATHER				
							Dir	Force	Barometer	Conditions	Sky	Vis	Temp

Maintenance and Reminders _____

_____

Fuel taken on _____ gals _____ gals

Water taken on _____ gals _____ gals

Passage from _____ **to** _____

ENGINE OR SAIL COMBINATION	REMARKS, COMMENTS, AND OBSERVATIONS

Persons on board _____

Log of the Yacht

Day of the week _____ Date _____

TIME	POSITION	COURSE	NAVIGATOR'S CHOICE	PERSON AT HELM	SKIPPER'S CHOICE	CURRENT	WIND		WEATHER				
							Dir	Force	Barometer	Conditions	Sky	Vis	Temp

Maintenance and Reminders _____

_____

Fuel taken on _____ gals _____ gals

Water taken on _____ gals _____ gals

Passage from _____ **to** _____

ENGINE OR SAIL COMBINATION	REMARKS, COMMENTS, AND OBSERVATIONS

Persons on board _____

Log of the Yacht _____ Day of the week _____ Date _____ _____

TIME	POSITION	COURSE	NAVIGATOR'S CHOICE	PERSON AT HELM	SKIPPER'S CHOICE	CURRENT	WIND		WEATHER				
							Dir	Force	Barometer	Conditions	Sky	Vis	Temp

Maintenance and Reminders _____   Fuel taken on _____ gals _____ gals

_____   Water taken on _____ gals _____ gals

Passage from _____ **to** _____

ENGINE OR SAIL COMBINATION	REMARKS, COMMENTS, AND OBSERVATIONS

Persons on board _____

Log of the Yacht

Day of the week _____ Date _____

TIME	POSITION	COURSE	NAVIGATOR'S CHOICE	PERSON AT HELM	SKIPPER'S CHOICE	CURRENT	WIND		WEATHER				
							Dir	Force	Barometer	Conditions	Sky	Vis	Temp

Maintenance and Reminders _____

Fuel taken on _____ gals _____ gals

Water taken on _____ gals _____ gals

Passage from _____ **to** _____

ENGINE OR SAIL COMBINATION	REMARKS, COMMENTS, AND OBSERVATIONS

Persons on board _____

Log of the Yacht

_____ Day of the week _____ Date _____

TIME	POSITION	COURSE	NAVIGATOR'S CHOICE	PERSON AT HELM	SKIPPER'S CHOICE	CURRENT	WIND		WEATHER				
							Dir	Force	Barometer	Conditions	Sky	Vis	Temp

Maintenance and Reminders _____   Fuel taken on _____ gals _____ gals

_____   Water taken on _____ gals _____ gals

Passage from _____ **to** _____

ENGINE OR SAIL COMBINATION	REMARKS, COMMENTS, AND OBSERVATIONS

Persons on board _____

Log of the Yacht _____ Day of the week _____ Date _____

TIME	POSITION	COURSE	NAVIGATOR'S CHOICE	PERSON AT HELM	SKIPPER'S CHOICE	CURRENT	WIND		WEATHER				
							Dir	Force	Barometer	Conditions	Sky	Vis	Temp

Maintenance and Reminders _____   Fuel taken on _____ gals _____ gals

_____   Water taken on _____ gals _____ gals

Passage from _____ **to** _____

ENGINE OR SAIL COMBINATION	REMARKS, COMMENTS, AND OBSERVATIONS

Persons on board _____

Log of the Yacht _____ Day of the week _____ Date _____

TIME	POSITION	COURSE	NAVIGATOR'S CHOICE	PERSON AT HELM	SKIPPER'S CHOICE	CURRENT	WIND		WEATHER				
							Dir	Force	Barometer	Conditions	Sky	Vis	Temp

Maintenance and Reminders _____ Fuel taken on _____ gals _____ gals

_____ Water taken on _____ gals _____ gals

Passage from _____ **to** _____

ENGINE OR SAIL COMBINATION	REMARKS, COMMENTS, AND OBSERVATIONS

Persons on board _____

Log of the Yacht ＿＿＿＿＿＿＿＿＿＿＿ Day of the week ＿＿＿＿＿＿ Date ＿＿＿＿＿＿

TIME	POSITION	COURSE	NAVIGATOR'S CHOICE	PERSON AT HELM	SKIPPER'S CHOICE	CURRENT	WIND		WEATHER				
							Dir	Force	Barometer	Conditions	Sky	Vis	Temp

Maintenance and Reminders ＿＿＿＿＿＿＿＿＿＿＿＿＿＿＿＿ Fuel taken on ＿＿＿＿ gals ＿＿＿＿ gals

＿＿＿＿＿＿＿＿＿＿＿＿＿＿＿＿＿＿＿＿＿＿＿＿＿＿＿ Water taken on ＿＿＿＿ gals ＿＿＿＿ gals

Passage from _____ **to** _____

ENGINE OR SAIL COMBINATION	REMARKS, COMMENTS, AND OBSERVATIONS

Persons on board _____

Log of the Yacht _____ Day of the week _____ Date _____

TIME	POSITION	COURSE	NAVIGATOR'S CHOICE	PERSON AT HELM	SKIPPER'S CHOICE	CURRENT	WIND		WEATHER				
							Dir	Force	Barometer	Conditions	Sky	Vis	Temp

Maintenance and Reminders _____ Fuel taken on _____ gals _____ gals

_____ Water taken on _____ gals _____ gals

Passage from _____ **to** _____

ENGINE OR SAIL COMBINATION	REMARKS, COMMENTS, AND OBSERVATIONS

Persons on board _____

Log of the Yacht _____ Day of the week _____ Date _____

TIME	POSITION	COURSE	NAVIGATOR'S CHOICE	PERSON AT HELM	SKIPPER'S CHOICE	CURRENT	WIND		WEATHER				
							Dir	Force	Barometer	Conditions	Sky	Vis	Temp

Maintenance and Reminders _____   Fuel taken on _____ gals _____ gals

_____   Water taken on _____ gals _____ gals

Passage from _____ **to** _____

ENGINE OR SAIL COMBINATION	REMARKS, COMMENTS, AND OBSERVATIONS

Persons on board _____

Log of the Yacht _____ Day of the week _____ Date _____

TIME	POSITION	COURSE	NAVIGATOR'S CHOICE	PERSON AT HELM	SKIPPER'S CHOICE	CURRENT	WIND		WEATHER				
							Dir	Force	Barometer	Conditions	Sky	Vis	Temp

Maintenance and Reminders _____

_____

Fuel taken on _____ gals _____ gals

Water taken on _____ gals _____ gals

Passage from _____ **to** _____

ENGINE OR SAIL COMBINATION	REMARKS, COMMENTS, AND OBSERVATIONS

Persons on board _____

Log of the Yacht _____ Day of the week _____ Date _____

TIME	POSITION	COURSE	NAVIGATOR'S CHOICE	PERSON AT HELM	SKIPPER'S CHOICE	CURRENT	WIND		WEATHER				
							Dir	Force	Barometer	Conditions	Sky	Vis	Temp

Maintenance and Reminders _____ Fuel taken on _____ gals _____ gals

_____ Water taken on _____ gals _____ gals

Passage from _____ **to** _____

ENGINE OR SAIL COMBINATION	REMARKS, COMMENTS, AND OBSERVATIONS

Persons on board _____

Log of the Yacht ———————————— Day of the week ———————— Date ————————

TIME	POSITION	COURSE	NAVIGATOR'S CHOICE	PERSON AT HELM	SKIPPER'S CHOICE	CURRENT	WIND		WEATHER				
							Dir	Force	Barometer	Conditions	Sky	Vis	Temp

Maintenance and Reminders ————————————————————   Fuel taken on ———— gals ———— gals

———————————————————————————   Water taken on ———— gals ———— gals

Passage from _____ **to** _____

ENGINE OR SAIL COMBINATION	REMARKS, COMMENTS, AND OBSERVATIONS

Persons on board _____

Log of the Yacht _____ Day of the week _____ Date _____

TIME	POSITION	COURSE	NAVIGATOR'S CHOICE	PERSON AT HELM	SKIPPER'S CHOICE	CURRENT	WIND		WEATHER				
							Dir	Force	Barometer	Conditions	Sky	Vis	Temp

Maintenance and Reminders _____   Fuel taken on _____ gals _____ gals

_____   Water taken on _____ gals _____ gals

Passage from _____ **to** _____

ENGINE OR SAIL COMBINATION	REMARKS, COMMENTS, AND OBSERVATIONS

Persons on board _____

Log of the Yacht _____ Day of the week _____ Date _____

TIME	POSITION	COURSE	NAVIGATOR'S CHOICE	PERSON AT HELM	SKIPPER'S CHOICE	CURRENT	WIND		WEATHER				
							Dir	Force	Barometer	Conditions	Sky	Vis	Temp

Maintenance and Reminders _____   Fuel taken on _____ gals _____ gals

_____   Water taken on _____ gals _____ gals

Passage from _____ **to** _____

ENGINE OR SAIL COMBINATION	REMARKS, COMMENTS, AND OBSERVATIONS

Persons on board _____

Log of the Yacht _____ Day of the week _____ Date _____

TIME	POSITION	COURSE	NAVIGATOR'S CHOICE	PERSON AT HELM	SKIPPER'S CHOICE	CURRENT	WIND		WEATHER				
							Dir	Force	Barometer	Conditions	Sky	Vis	Temp

Maintenance and Reminders _____   Fuel taken on _____ gals _____ gals

_____   Water taken on _____ gals _____ gals

Passage from _____ **to** _____

ENGINE OR SAIL COMBINATION	REMARKS, COMMENTS, AND OBSERVATIONS

Persons on board _____

Log of the Yacht

Day of the week _____ Date _____

TIME	POSITION	COURSE	NAVIGATOR'S CHOICE	PERSON AT HELM	SKIPPER'S CHOICE	CURRENT	WIND		WEATHER				
							Dir	Force	Barometer	Conditions	Sky	Vis	Temp

Maintenance and Reminders _____   Fuel taken on _____ gals _____ gals

_____   Water taken on _____ gals _____ gals

Passage from _____ **to** _____

ENGINE OR SAIL COMBINATION	REMARKS, COMMENTS, AND OBSERVATIONS

Persons on board _____

Log of the Yacht _____ Day of the week _____ Date _____

TIME	POSITION	COURSE	NAVIGATOR'S CHOICE	PERSON AT HELM	SKIPPER'S CHOICE	CURRENT	WIND		WEATHER				
							Dir	Force	Barometer	Conditions	Sky	Vis	Temp

Maintenance and Reminders _____   Fuel taken on _____ gals _____ gals

_____   Water taken on _____ gals _____ gals

Passage from _____ **to** _____

ENGINE OR SAIL COMBINATION	REMARKS, COMMENTS, AND OBSERVATIONS

Persons on board _____

Log of the Yacht _____ Day of the week _____ Date _____

TIME	POSITION	COURSE	NAVIGATOR'S CHOICE	PERSON AT HELM	SKIPPER'S CHOICE	CURRENT	WIND		WEATHER				
							Dir	Force	Barometer	Conditions	Sky	Vis	Temp

Maintenance and Reminders _____   Fuel taken on _____ gals _____ gals

_____   Water taken on _____ gals _____ gals

Passage from _____ **to** _____

ENGINE OR SAIL COMBINATION	REMARKS, COMMENTS, AND OBSERVATIONS

Persons on board _____

Log of the Yacht _____ Day of the week _____ Date _____

TIME	POSITION	COURSE	NAVIGATOR'S CHOICE	PERSON AT HELM	SKIPPER'S CHOICE	CURRENT	WIND		WEATHER				
							Dir	Force	Barometer	Conditions	Sky	Vis	Temp

Maintenance and Reminders _____ Fuel taken on _____ gals _____ gals

_____ Water taken on _____ gals _____ gals

Passage from _____ **to** _____

ENGINE OR SAIL COMBINATION	REMARKS, COMMENTS, AND OBSERVATIONS

Persons on board _____

Log of the Yacht _____ Day of the week _____ Date _____

TIME	POSITION	COURSE	NAVIGATOR'S CHOICE	PERSON AT HELM	SKIPPER'S CHOICE	CURRENT	WIND		WEATHER				
							Dir	Force	Barometer	Conditions	Sky	Vis	Temp

Maintenance and Reminders _____   Fuel taken on _____ gals _____ gals

_____   Water taken on _____ gals _____ gals

Passage from _____ **to** _____

ENGINE OR SAIL COMBINATION	REMARKS, COMMENTS, AND OBSERVATIONS

Persons on board _____

Log of the Yacht _____ Day of the week _____ Date _____

TIME	POSITION	COURSE	NAVIGATOR'S CHOICE	PERSON AT HELM	SKIPPER'S CHOICE	CURRENT	WIND		WEATHER				
							Dir	Force	Barometer	Conditions	Sky	Vis	Temp

Maintenance and Reminders _____ Fuel taken on _____ gals _____ gals

_____ Water taken on _____ gals _____ gals

Passage from _____ **to** _____

ENGINE OR SAIL COMBINATION	REMARKS, COMMENTS, AND OBSERVATIONS

Persons on board _____

Log of the Yacht _____ Day of the week _____ Date _____

TIME	POSITION	COURSE	NAVIGATOR'S CHOICE	PERSON AT HELM	SKIPPER'S CHOICE	CURRENT	WIND		WEATHER				
							Dir	Force	Barometer	Conditions	Sky	Vis	Temp

Maintenance and Reminders _____

Fuel taken on _____ gals _____ gals

Water taken on _____ gals _____ gals

Passage from _____ **to** _____

ENGINE OR SAIL COMBINATION	REMARKS, COMMENTS, AND OBSERVATIONS

Persons on board _____

Log of the Yacht _____ Day of the week _____ Date _____

TIME	POSITION	COURSE	NAVIGATOR'S CHOICE	PERSON AT HELM	SKIPPER'S CHOICE	CURRENT	WIND		WEATHER				
							Dir	Force	Barometer	Conditions	Sky	Vis	Temp

Maintenance and Reminders _____   Fuel taken on _____ gals _____ gals

_____   Water taken on _____ gals _____ gals

Passage from _____ **to** _____

ENGINE OR SAIL COMBINATION	REMARKS, COMMENTS, AND OBSERVATIONS

Persons on board _____

Log of the Yacht _____ Day of the week _____ Date _____

TIME	POSITION	COURSE	NAVIGATOR'S CHOICE	PERSON AT HELM	SKIPPER'S CHOICE	CURRENT	WIND		WEATHER				
							Dir	Force	Barometer	Conditions	Sky	Vis	Temp

Maintenance and Reminders _____   Fuel taken on _____ gals _____ gals

_____   Water taken on _____ gals _____ gals

Passage from _____ **to** _____

ENGINE OR SAIL COMBINATION	REMARKS, COMMENTS, AND OBSERVATIONS

Persons on board _____

Log of the Yacht _____ Day of the week _____ Date _____

TIME	POSITION	COURSE	NAVIGATOR'S CHOICE	PERSON AT HELM	SKIPPER'S CHOICE	CURRENT	WIND		WEATHER				
							Dir	Force	Barometer	Conditions	Sky	Vis	Temp

Maintenance and Reminders _____

_____

Fuel taken on _____ gals _____ gals

Water taken on _____ gals _____ gals

Passage from _____ **to** _____

ENGINE OR SAIL COMBINATION	REMARKS, COMMENTS, AND OBSERVATIONS

Persons on board _____

Log of the Yacht _____ Day of the week _____ Date _____

TIME	POSITION	COURSE	NAVIGATOR'S CHOICE	PERSON AT HELM	SKIPPER'S CHOICE	CURRENT	WIND		WEATHER				
							Dir	Force	Barometer	Conditions	Sky	Vis	Temp

Maintenance and Reminders _____ Fuel taken on _____ gals _____ gals

_____ Water taken on _____ gals _____ gals

Passage from _____ **to** _____

ENGINE OR SAIL COMBINATION	REMARKS, COMMENTS, AND OBSERVATIONS

Persons on board _____

Log of the Yacht _____ Day of the week _____ Date _____

TIME	POSITION	COURSE	NAVIGATOR'S CHOICE	PERSON AT HELM	SKIPPER'S CHOICE	CURRENT	WIND		WEATHER				
							Dir	Force	Barometer	Conditions	Sky	Vis	Temp

Maintenance and Reminders _____

_____

Fuel taken on _____ gals _____ gals

Water taken on _____ gals _____ gals

Passage from _____ **to** _____

ENGINE OR SAIL COMBINATION	REMARKS, COMMENTS, AND OBSERVATIONS

Persons on board _____

Log of the Yacht _____ Day of the week _____ Date _____

TIME	POSITION	COURSE	NAVIGATOR'S CHOICE	PERSON AT HELM	SKIPPER'S CHOICE	CURRENT	WIND		WEATHER				
							Dir	Force	Barometer	Conditions	Sky	Vis	Temp

Maintenance and Reminders _____

Fuel taken on _____ gals _____ gals

Water taken on _____ gals _____ gals

Passage from _____ **to** _____

ENGINE OR SAIL COMBINATION	REMARKS, COMMENTS, AND OBSERVATIONS

Persons on board _____

Log of the Yacht _____ Day of the week _____ Date _____

TIME	POSITION	COURSE	NAVIGATOR'S CHOICE	PERSON AT HELM	SKIPPER'S CHOICE	CURRENT	WIND		WEATHER				
							Dir	Force	Barometer	Conditions	Sky	Vis	Temp

Maintenance and Reminders _____   Fuel taken on _____ gals _____ gals

_____   Water taken on _____ gals _____ gals

Passage from _____ **to** _____

ENGINE OR SAIL COMBINATION	REMARKS, COMMENTS, AND OBSERVATIONS

Persons on board _____

Log of the Yacht _____ Day of the week _____ Date _____

TIME	POSITION	COURSE	NAVIGATOR'S CHOICE	PERSON AT HELM	SKIPPER'S CHOICE	CURRENT	WIND		WEATHER				
							Dir	Force	Barometer	Conditions	Sky	Vis	Temp

Maintenance and Reminders _____ Fuel taken on _____ gals _____ gals

_____ Water taken on _____ gals _____ gals

Passage from _____ **to** _____

ENGINE OR SAIL COMBINATION	REMARKS, COMMENTS, AND OBSERVATIONS

Persons on board _____

Log of the Yacht _____   Day of the week _____   Date _____

TIME	POSITION	COURSE	NAVIGATOR'S CHOICE	PERSON AT HELM	SKIPPER'S CHOICE	CURRENT	WIND		WEATHER				
							Dir	Force	Barometer	Conditions	Sky	Vis	Temp

Maintenance and Reminders _____   Fuel taken on _____ gals _____ gals

_____   Water taken on _____ gals _____ gals

Passage from _____ **to** _____

ENGINE OR SAIL COMBINATION	REMARKS, COMMENTS, AND OBSERVATIONS

Persons on board _____

Log of the Yacht _____ Day of the week _____ Date _____

TIME	POSITION	COURSE	NAVIGATOR'S CHOICE	PERSON AT HELM	SKIPPER'S CHOICE	CURRENT	WIND		WEATHER				
							Dir	Force	Barometer	Conditions	Sky	Vis	Temp

Maintenance and Reminders _____ Fuel taken on _____ gals _____ gals

_____ Water taken on _____ gals _____ gals

Passage from _____ **to** _____

ENGINE OR SAIL COMBINATION	REMARKS, COMMENTS, AND OBSERVATIONS

Persons on board _____

Log of the Yacht _____ Day of the week _____ Date _____

TIME	POSITION	COURSE	NAVIGATOR'S CHOICE	PERSON AT HELM	SKIPPER'S CHOICE	CURRENT	WIND		WEATHER				
							Dir	Force	Barometer	Conditions	Sky	Vis	Temp

Maintenance and Reminders _____

_____

Fuel taken on _____ gals _____ gals

Water taken on _____ gals _____ gals

Passage from _____ **to** _____

ENGINE OR SAIL COMBINATION	REMARKS, COMMENTS, AND OBSERVATIONS

Persons on board _____

Log of the Yacht _____ Day of the week _____ Date _____

TIME	POSITION	COURSE	NAVIGATOR'S CHOICE	PERSON AT HELM	SKIPPER'S CHOICE	CURRENT	WIND		WEATHER				
							Dir	Force	Barometer	Conditions	Sky	Vis	Temp

Maintenance and Reminders _____ Fuel taken on _____ gals _____ gals

Water taken on _____ gals _____ gals

Passage from _____ **to** _____

ENGINE OR SAIL COMBINATION	REMARKS, COMMENTS, AND OBSERVATIONS

Persons on board _____

Log of the Yacht _____ Day of the week _____ Date _____

TIME	POSITION	COURSE	NAVIGATOR'S CHOICE	PERSON AT HELM	SKIPPER'S CHOICE	CURRENT	WIND		WEATHER				
							Dir	Force	Barometer	Conditions	Sky	Vis	Temp

Maintenance and Reminders _____   Fuel taken on _____ gals _____ gals

_____   Water taken on _____ gals _____ gals

Passage from _____ **to** _____

ENGINE OR SAIL COMBINATION	REMARKS, COMMENTS, AND OBSERVATIONS

Persons on board _____

Log of the Yacht _____ Day of the week _____ Date _____

TIME	POSITION	COURSE	NAVIGATOR'S CHOICE	PERSON AT HELM	SKIPPER'S CHOICE	CURRENT	WIND		WEATHER				
							Dir	Force	Barometer	Conditions	Sky	Vis	Temp

Maintenance and Reminders _____   Fuel taken on _____ gals _____ gals

_____   Water taken on _____ gals _____ gals

Passage from _____ **to** _____

ENGINE OR SAIL COMBINATION	REMARKS, COMMENTS, AND OBSERVATIONS

Persons on board _____

Log of the Yacht _____ Day of the week _____ Date _____

TIME	POSITION	COURSE	NAVIGATOR'S CHOICE	PERSON AT HELM	SKIPPER'S CHOICE	CURRENT	WIND		WEATHER				
							Dir	Force	Barometer	Conditions	Sky	Vis	Temp

Maintenance and Reminders _____

_____

Fuel taken on _____ gals _____ gals

Water taken on _____ gals _____ gals

Passage from _____ **to** _____

ENGINE OR SAIL COMBINATION	REMARKS, COMMENTS, AND OBSERVATIONS

Persons on board _____

Log of the Yacht _____ Day of the week _____ Date _____

TIME	POSITION	COURSE	NAVIGATOR'S CHOICE	PERSON AT HELM	SKIPPER'S CHOICE	CURRENT	WIND		WEATHER				
							Dir	Force	Barometer	Conditions	Sky	Vis	Temp

Maintenance and Reminders _____   Fuel taken on _____ gals _____ gals

_____   Water taken on _____ gals _____ gals

Passage from _____ **to** _____

ENGINE OR SAIL COMBINATION	REMARKS, COMMENTS, AND OBSERVATIONS

Persons on board _____

Log of the Yacht _____ Day of the week _____ Date _____

TIME	POSITION	COURSE	NAVIGATOR'S CHOICE	PERSON AT HELM	SKIPPER'S CHOICE	CURRENT	WIND		WEATHER				
							Dir	Force	Barometer	Conditions	Sky	Vis	Temp

Maintenance and Reminders _____

_____

Fuel taken on _____ gals _____ gals

Water taken on _____ gals _____ gals

Passage from _____ to _____

ENGINE OR SAIL COMBINATION	REMARKS, COMMENTS, AND OBSERVATIONS

Persons on board _____

Radio log

Boat Name _____ Year _____ Call Letters _____

DATE	TIME	CALL		POWER		OPERATOR	VESSEL OR STATION	CHANNEL		CALL LETTERS	PURPOSE
		Rec.	Xmit	Hi	Low			Call	Shift		

Radio log

Boat Name _____ Year _____ Call Letters _____

DATE	TIME	CALL		POWER		OPERATOR	VESSEL OR STATION	CHANNEL		CALL LETTERS	PURPOSE
		Rec.	Xmit	Hi	Low			Call	Shift		

Radio log

Boat Name _____ Year _____ Call Letters _____

DATE	TIME	CALL		POWER		OPERATOR	VESSEL OR STATION	CHANNEL		CALL LETTERS	PURPOSE
		Rec.	Xmit	Hi	Low			Call	Shift		